TURTLES WERE NAMED AFTER THEM!

LEONARDO, DONATELLO, RAPHAEL AND MICHELANGELO

BIOGRAPHY FOR KIDS 6-8
CHILDREN'S BIOGRAPHY BOOKS

BABY PROFESSOR
EDUCATION KIDS

Speedy Publishing LLC
40 E. Main St. #1156
Newark, DE 19711
www.speedypublishing.com
Copyright 2017

In this book, we're going to talk about the famous artists Leonardo, Donatello, Raphael, and Michelangelo. So, let's get right to it!

The Renaissance Period in Italy was a time when many great painters and sculptors thrived. Although their work took place many centuries ago, it's still a major source of inspiration for artists today.

Leonardo Da Vinci

LEONARDO DA VINCI
(1452 through 1519 AD)

Many people know about Leonardo da Vinci from his famous painting, the *Mona Lisa,* which is now hanging in the Louvre museum in Paris. Today, we would call Leonardo the perfect "Renaissance Man." This term means someone who excels in many areas and has many different talents. Leonardo was an innovator in art, science, and architecture.

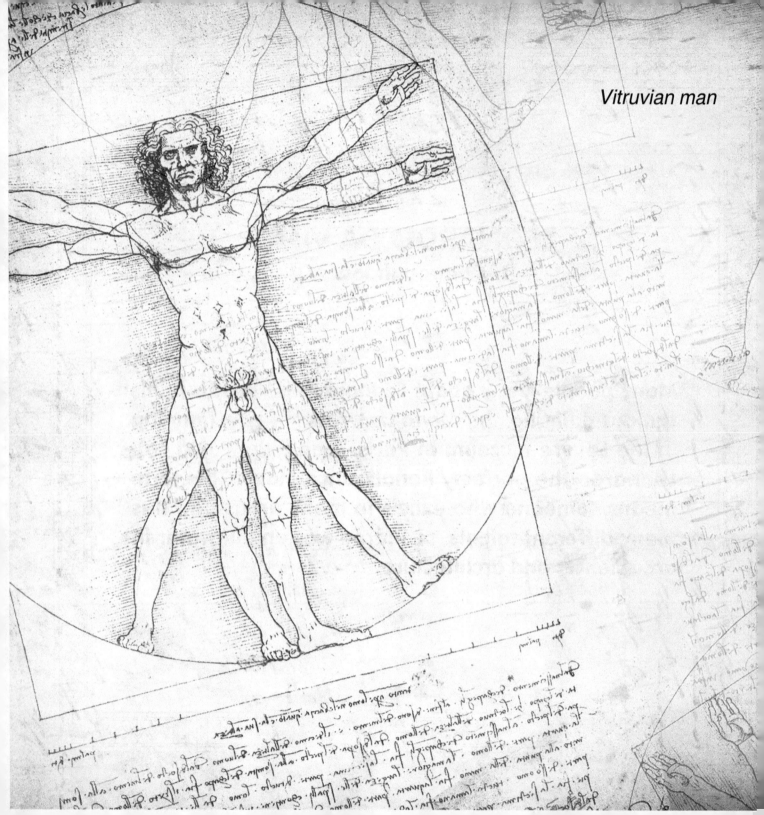

Vitruvian man

He studied the human anatomy in detail and used his knowledge when he created paintings and sculptures.

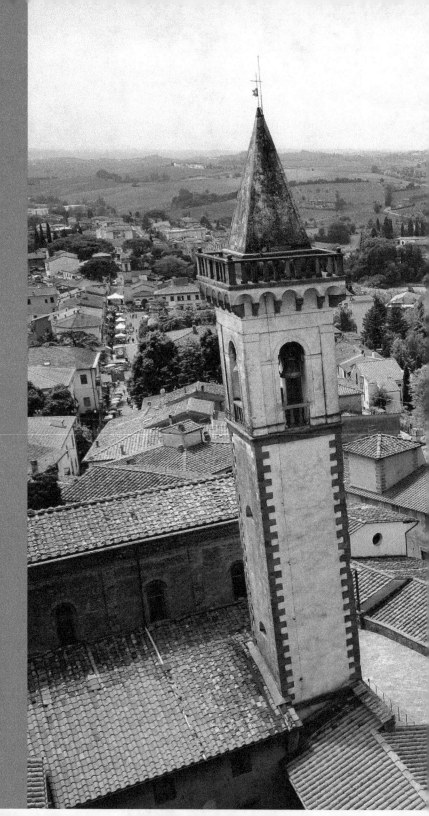

Leonardo was born in the city of Vinci, Italy in 1452. His father, Ser Piero, was an important notary for attorneys, but his mother was a peasant girl who wasn't married to his father. Ser Piero raised him along with the help of more than one stepmother.

Portrait of Perugino

Surprisingly, Leonardo didn't receive much of a formal education. However, his art skill showed up very early in his life. When Leonardo was still a teenager, his father sent him to work with master painter and sculptor Andrea del Verrocchio of Florence. He remained at Verrocchio's workshop until he was ready to go out on his own as an independent master artist in 1478, when he was 26 years old.

Leonardo painted the *Last Supper,* one of his most famous works, on the wall of a convent in Milan, Italy. It took him seven years to complete the painting. It was painted in a room called the refectory where the Dominican nuns would meet together to have their meals. This mural painting depicts the moment when Jesus told the apostles that he would be betrayed by one of them soon. Leonardo used a new technique he had created to paint the wall in layers and unfortunately his experiment didn't work. His masterpiece began to deteriorate during his lifetime and has undergone a great deal of restoration. The most recent restoration took place from 1979 to 1999.

Monalisa Portrait

Around 1503 AD, Leonardo was commissioned to do a portrait. Most historians believe the portrait was supposed to be Lisa del Gioconda, who was the wife of a wealthy merchant who sold silks. However, this isn't certain, and many have speculated that the portrait might not even be based on any particular model. It became Leonardo's favorite painting and he didn't give it up. He kept it with him until he died and willed it to one of his pupils. It was sold to the King of France for 4,000 gold coins. Today, this world-famous painting, the *Mona Lisa,* is estimated to be worth over 1 billion dollars and is shown behind bulletproof glass in the Louvre museum in Paris.

Donatello

DONATELLO
(1386 through 1466 AD)

Donatello's full name was Donato di Niccolò di Betto Bardi and he was born in 1386 AD. Donatello's father was a craftsman so Donatello was able to become an apprentice to masterful sculptors in his youth. He was very talented and began receiving commissions for art by the age of 20.

In 1408, at the workshops of a cathedral in Florence, he completed a life-size sculpture of *David,* from the biblical story of David and Goliath. He used a Gothic style, which was popular at the time. This style featured a face that didn't show an expression and long, flowing lines with draped fabrics. It's beautifully executed but isn't like Donatello's later, more innovative works.

Sculpture of David

Although the statue was meant to be displayed in the cathedral it was placed in the town hall of Florence called the Palazzo Vecchio. It became a symbol for the Florentine people of their defiance against the authority of the king of Naples.

Cosimo de' Medici Portrait

Donatello became friends with banker and politician Cosimo de' Medici. The Medici family was very powerful and influential and this helped Donatello's career.

Sculpture of Niccolò da Uzzano

In the year 1430, Cosimo commissioned Donatello to do another *David.* This statue in bronze turned out to be one of Donatello's most famous masterpieces. It was the first Renaissance statue created from bronze cast that could stand on its own without any support. It was also the first nude male sculpture that had been created since ancient times. It was controversial at the time, which simply means that some people loved it and others didn't like it at all.

In 1443, Donatello was commissioned to do a statue of Erasmo da Narni. Donatello completed the statue in 1450. This bronze statue called *Gattamelata* shows Erasmo, who was a soldier, dressed for battle and riding a horse. This statue also created controversy since in those days most statues with horses were reserved for kings.

In 1455, he completed another masterpiece. It was a wooden statue called *Magdalene Penitent,* which was a representation of Mary Magdalene from the New Testament. It was a very realistic statue showing a woman who had wasted away in the desert.

Throughout his lifetime of work, Donatello found new ways to show perspective in his sculptures. He was influenced by the sculptures of the early Greeks and Romans that emphasized human forms and events.

Raphael

RAPHAEL
(1483 through 1520 AD)

Raphael's full name was Raffaello Sanzio and he was born in the city of Urbino, Italy in 1483. The arts were encouraged in Urbino and the young Raphael was taught by his father Giovanni Santi, who was painting for his patron, the Duke of Urbino.

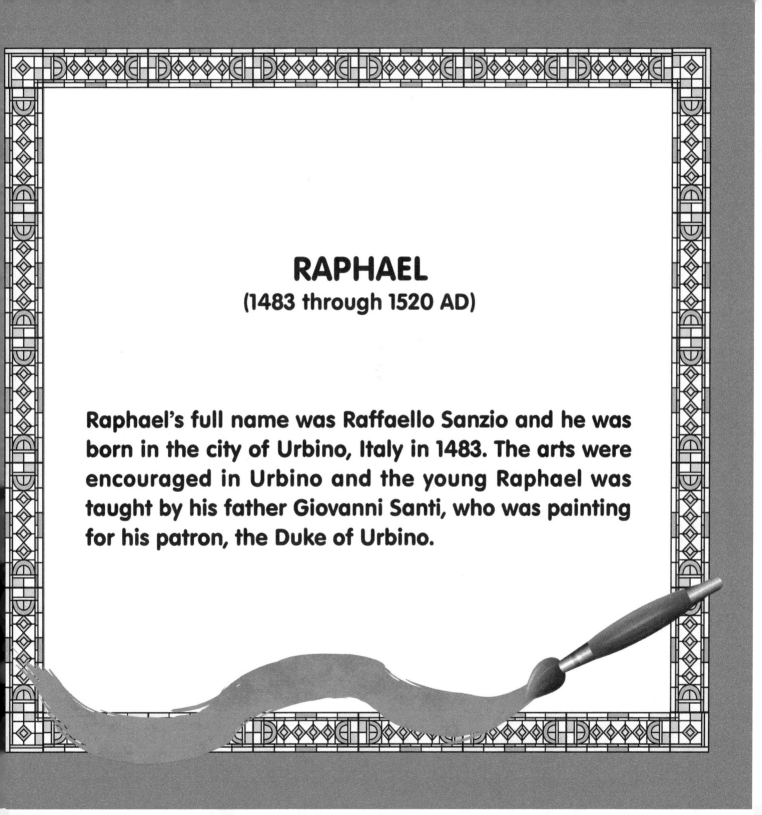

In 1500, the master painter Perugino invited the young Raphael to come to his workshop and become an apprentice in the city of Perugia in central Italy. Raphael's apprenticeship lasted four years and he soaked up as much knowledge as possible.

Lorenzo Perugino

In 1504, he moved to Florence, where he came under the spell of other Italian painters such as Leonardo da Vinci and Michelangelo. He was so excited by their works and studied them so he could achieve a more expressive style than was shown in his earlier work.

Pope Julius II hired Raphael to paint rooms in the Vatican beginning in 1508. Raphael and his team of other artists labored to create these fresco cycles.

Fresco was a style of painting on wet plaster and these frescoes were done in cycles, which simply means they told a story in each panel, one after the other.

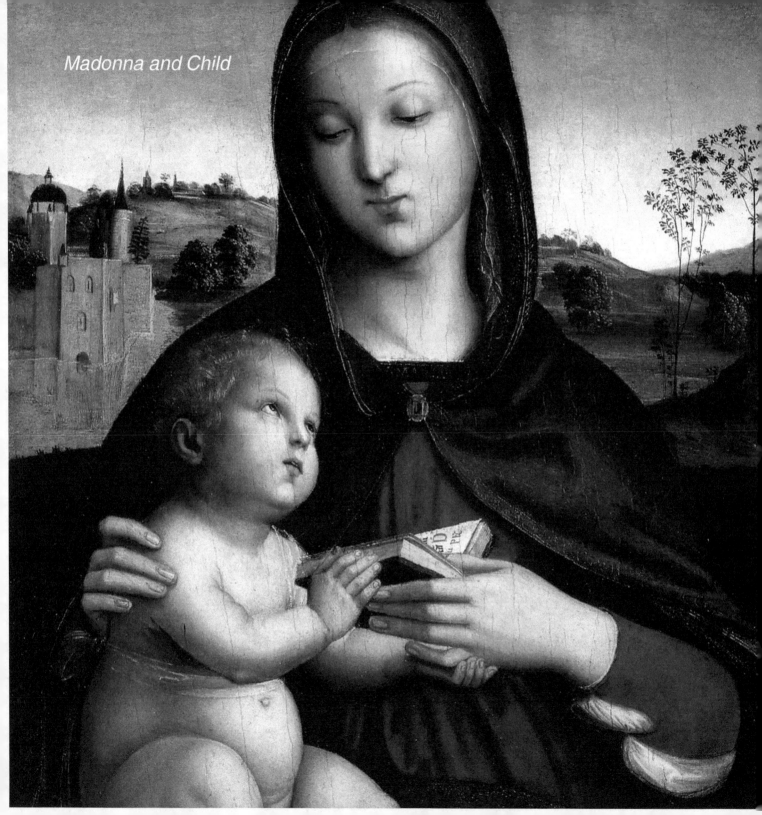

Madonna and Child

By 1514, Raphael had become famous for his paintings in the Vatican. During his short lifetime, Raphael painted hundreds of paintings, mostly of religious subjects such as angels and the Virgin Mary with the baby Jesus. He was also commissioned for many portraits. His paintings were known for their perfect details. Sadly, he died at the age of 37 and the cause of his death isn't fully known.

Michelangelo

MICHELANGELO
(1475 through 1564 AD)

Michelangelo Buonarroti was born in 1475 in the city of Caprese, Italy. Shortly after he was born, his family moved to Florence and Michelangelo would always consider this art-centered city his true home.

His talent for both sculpting and painting quickly grabbed the attention of Lorenzo de' Medici of the powerful Medici family, who were bankers and politicians. For a period of time, Michelangelo lived in their palace-like home.

Lorenzo De Medici

Michelangelo was in Rome in 1498 and while there he received an important commission. It was for creating a large statue of a seated Virgin Mary holding the crucified Christ in her arms. The statue was to be made of marble and be placed at the entrance of the future tomb of Jean Bilhères de Lagraulas, who was a French cardinal and the French king's representative to the pope.

Michelangelo carved the massive statue out of one block of marble and it is one of the world's most enduring masterpieces called the Pietà. Throngs of visitors come to see it at St. Peter's Basilica every year.

In 1501, he created the figure of *David* from the Old Testament. This massive sculpture at 17 feet tall shows an energetic and powerful young man ready to take on a giant. This masterpiece has become a symbol for the city of Florence.

In 1508, Pope Julius II commissioned Michelangelo to paint the Sistine Chapel's ceiling with images of the apostles. Instead, Michelangelo painted story scenes from the Old Testament in an intricate pattern of clothed and unclothed figures. The most famous of the paintings shows a depiction of God reaching out to give Adam life.

Michelangelo considered himself a sculptor not a painter

and yet he created one of the most famous paintings in the world.

If you've ever heard the names Leonardo, Donatello, Raphael, and Michelangelo used together before, you might be thinking of the Teenage Mutant Ninja Turtles. They were named after the Renaissance artists. They are four fictional turtles who act like human teenagers. They were first drawn for comic books and then merchandised into a cartoon series, video games, and toys. They were part of popular culture in the 1980s and 90s and have become popular again over the last few years.

Awesome! Now you know more about the famous artists Leonardo, Donatello, Raphael, and Michelangelo. You can find more Biography books from Baby Professor by searching the website of your favorite book retailer.

Visit

BABY PROFESSOR
EDUCATION KIDS

www.BabyProfessorBooks.com
to download Free Baby Professor eBooks
and view our catalog of new and exciting
Children's Books

CPSIA information can be obtained
at www.ICGtesting.com
Printed in the USA
BVHW091254020622
638621BV00004B/223

9 781541 914117